The Innovator's Mind Cultivating Creativity for Breakthrough Ideas

farisa

The Innovator's Mind Cultivating Creativity for Breakthrough Ideas

Copyright © 2023 by farisa

The first edition was published in 2023

ISBN:

Published by:
Sunshine
1663 Liberty Drive
Hyderabad, IN 47403
www.Sunshinepublishers.com

This book is self-published using on-demand printing and publishing, which allows it to be printed and distributed globally

TABLE OF CONTENT

Chapter 1: Understanding Creativity and Innovation

The Importance of Creativity in Today's World

Defining Creativity and Innovation

The Connection between Creativity and Innovation

Debunking Common Myths About Creativity

Embracing a Growth Mindset

Overcoming Fear of Failure

Cultivating Curiosity and Openness

Nurturing a Positive Attitude towards Change

Tapping into Your Imagination

Developing Critical Thinking Skills

Enhancing Problem-Solving Abilities

Stimulating Divergent Thinking

Chapter 1: Understanding Creativity and Innovation

The Importance of Creativity in Today's World

In today's fast-paced and ever-changing world, creativity has become a vital asset for individuals and organizations alike. In "The Innovator's Mind: Cultivating Creativity for Breakthrough Ideas," we delve into the significance of creativity and how it can be nurtured to unlock breakthrough ideas in various fields. This subchapter, "The Importance of Creativity in Today's World," aims to highlight the crucial role creativity plays in our lives and why it has become a key factor in achieving success.

In the book "Mindset: The New Psychology of Success," the concept of a growth mindset is explored, emphasizing the belief that intelligence and abilities can be developed through dedication and hard work. Creativity, in this context, is a fundamental aspect of a growth mindset, as it encourages individuals to think outside the box, challenge conventional thinking, and explore new possibilities.

In today's increasingly competitive world, creativity has become a differentiating factor. With automation and artificial intelligence taking over routine tasks, creativity is what sets us apart from machines. It enables us to find innovative solutions to complex problems, adapt to rapidly changing circumstances, and create new opportunities. Whether you are an entrepreneur, an artist, a scientist, or a student, creativity is essential for success in any field.

Moreover, creativity fosters a sense of curiosity, open-mindedness, and resilience. It encourages us to constantly seek new knowledge, embrace diverse perspectives, and overcome obstacles. By cultivating creativity, we not only enhance our problem-solving abilities but also develop a flexible mindset that allows us to adapt and thrive in an ever-evolving world.

Furthermore, creativity fuels innovation, driving economic growth and societal progress. It is the catalyst for groundbreaking inventions, revolutionary technologies, and transformative ideas that shape our future. From the development of life-saving medical treatments to the creation of sustainable energy solutions, creativity is at the core of human progress.

In conclusion, "The Innovator's Mind: Cultivating Creativity for Breakthrough Ideas" emphasizes the paramount importance of creativity in today's world. By fostering a growth mindset and nurturing our creative abilities, we can unlock our full potential, stand out in a competitive landscape, and contribute to the advancement of society. Whether you are an aspiring innovator, a lifelong learner, or anyone seeking success, embracing and harnessing the power of creativity is key to achieving breakthrough ideas and personal fulfillment.

Defining Creativity and Innovation

Creativity and innovation are words that are often used interchangeably, but they have distinct meanings and play different roles in the process of generating breakthrough ideas. In this subchapter, we will explore the definitions of creativity and innovation, and how they contribute to cultivating a mindset of success.

Creativity can be defined as the ability to generate novel and valuable ideas, solutions, or concepts. It involves thinking outside the box, breaking conventional patterns, and approaching problems from unique angles. Creativity is not limited to artistic endeavors; it can be applied to any field or aspect of life. Whether you are a scientist, entrepreneur, or educator, embracing creativity is essential for pushing boundaries and finding innovative solutions.

On the other hand, innovation refers to the process of implementing creative ideas into practical applications that provide value. It involves taking those novel concepts and turning them into tangible products, services, or processes that improve the lives of individuals or society as a whole. Innovation is about taking risks, experimenting, and iterating on ideas until they reach their full potential. It is the driving force behind progress and the catalyst for breakthroughs in various industries.

Understanding the difference between creativity and innovation is crucial for developing a growth mindset. The book "The Innovator's Mind: Cultivating Creativity for Breakthrough Ideas" delves into the psychology of success and highlights the importance of fostering both creativity and innovation in our lives. By adopting a growth mindset, we can embrace challenges, learn from failures, and continuously develop our creative abilities.

Moreover, cultivating a mindset of success involves recognizing that creativity and innovation are not fixed traits, but skills that can be nurtured and developed. The book emphasizes the power of deliberate practice, curiosity, and persistence in honing our creative thinking abilities. It provides practical strategies and exercises to enhance our creative problem-solving skills and embrace innovative thinking.

By delving into the subchapter "Defining Creativity and Innovation," readers from any background or niche can gain a deeper understanding of these concepts. Whether you are an aspiring entrepreneur seeking to develop groundbreaking products or an educator looking to foster creativity in your students, this subchapter serves as a foundational guide to unlocking the potential of creativity and innovation within yourself and your endeavors.

The Connection between Creativity and Innovation

In today's rapidly evolving world, creativity and innovation have become vital for success in any field. Whether you are an artist, entrepreneur, scientist, or educator, understanding the connection between creativity and innovation is crucial for cultivating breakthrough ideas. In this subchapter, we will explore how creativity and innovation are interconnected and how they can be harnessed to achieve remarkable results.

Creativity is the foundation on which innovation thrives. It is the ability to generate novel ideas, think outside the box, and approach problems from unique perspectives. A creative mindset allows individuals to challenge conventional thinking, break through barriers, and envision new possibilities. However, creativity alone is not enough to drive meaningful change; it is through innovation that creative ideas are transformed into practical solutions.

Innovation is the process of implementing creative ideas to create value. It involves taking risks, experimenting, and bringing ideas to life. Innovation requires a combination of creativity, resourcefulness, and perseverance. It is about turning imaginative concepts into tangible products, services, or processes that have a positive impact on individuals, organizations, and society as a whole.

The link between creativity and innovation is symbiotic. Creativity fuels innovation by providing a constant stream of fresh ideas, while innovation channels and amplifies the impact of creative thinking. Without creativity, innovation becomes stagnant, relying on repetitive solutions that fail to address emerging challenges. Conversely, without innovation, creativity remains confined to the realm of imagination, with ideas never materializing into tangible outcomes.

To cultivate creativity for breakthrough ideas, it is essential to adopt a growth mindset. In Carol S. Dweck's book "Mindset: The New Psychology of Success," she explores the power of a growth mindset, which is the belief that abilities can be developed through dedication and hard work. Embracing a growth mindset allows individuals to see failure as an opportunity for learning and growth, rather than a setback.

By fostering a growth mindset and nurturing creativity, individuals can unlock their innovative potential. This can be achieved by creating an environment that encourages experimentation, collaboration, and risk-taking. It is also vital to engage in activities that stimulate creativity, such as brainstorming sessions, exposure to diverse perspectives, and continuous learning.

In conclusion, creativity and innovation are inseparable partners in the quest for breakthrough ideas. By understanding the connection between creativity and innovation and cultivating a growth mindset, individuals can harness their creative potential to drive meaningful change and achieve remarkable success in their respective fields.

Debunking Common Myths About Creativity

Creativity is often seen as a mysterious and elusive quality that only a select few possess. However, in "The Innovator's Mind: Cultivating Creativity for Breakthrough Ideas," we aim to debunk common myths about creativity and show that it is a skill that can be cultivated by anyone.

Myth 1: Only artists and geniuses are creative. Contrary to popular belief, creativity is not limited to a specific group of individuals. It is a mindset and a set of skills that can be developed by anyone. While artists and geniuses may showcase their creativity in more visible ways, creativity can manifest itself in various forms, such as problem-solving, innovative thinking, and ideation. By embracing the belief that creativity is not exclusive to a select few, anyone can tap into their creative potential.

Myth 2: Creativity is all about inspiration and ideas. While inspiration and ideas play a crucial role in the creative process, they are only the starting point. Creativity is not solely about coming up with brilliant ideas; it is about taking action and turning those ideas into reality. It involves a combination of imagination, curiosity, and a willingness to take risks. By understanding that creativity is not just about ideas but also about execution, individuals can overcome the myth that creativity is unattainable for them.

Myth 3: Creativity is a random and unpredictable process. Many people believe that creativity is a random and unpredictable process that cannot be controlled. However, research has shown that creativity can be nurtured and cultivated through deliberate practice and a growth mindset. By adopting strategies such as brainstorming, seeking diverse perspectives, and experimenting with new approaches, individuals can enhance their creative thinking abilities. Understanding that creativity is a skill that can be developed over time allows individuals to take an active role in their creative journey.

Myth 4: Creativity is only for the "right-brained" individuals. The notion that creativity is exclusive to individuals with a dominant right hemisphere is a common misconception. In reality, creativity involves the integration of both the left and right brain hemispheres. It is a multidimensional process that combines logical thinking with imagination and intuition. By embracing the idea that creativity is not limited to specific brain functions, individuals can tap into their full creative potential regardless of their dominant hemisphere.

In conclusion, "The Innovator's Mind: Cultivating Creativity for Breakthrough Ideas" aims to debunk common myths surrounding creativity and empower individuals to cultivate their creative potential. By understanding that creativity is not limited to a select few, requires action and execution, can be developed through deliberate practice, and involves the integration of both brain hemispheres, anyone can embrace their creative abilities and unlock breakthrough ideas.

Chapter 2: The Innovator's Mindset: Developing a Creative Mind

Embracing a Growth Mindset

In the fast-paced world we live in today, it has become increasingly important to cultivate a growth mindset. In the book "The Innovator's Mind: Cultivating Creativity for Breakthrough Ideas," we explore the power of adopting a growth mindset and how it can lead to greater success and fulfillment in all areas of life.

What exactly is a growth mindset? Coined by psychologist Carol Dweck in her groundbreaking book "Mindset: The New Psychology of Success," a growth mindset refers to the belief that our abilities and intelligence can be developed through dedication, hard work, and a willingness to learn. In contrast, a fixed mindset is the belief that our qualities and abilities are fixed traits that cannot be changed.

By embracing a growth mindset, we open ourselves up to endless possibilities and opportunities for growth. We begin to view challenges as opportunities for learning and development rather than as obstacles to overcome. This mindset shift allows us to approach life with a sense of curiosity and resilience, knowing that failure is not indicative of our abilities but rather a stepping stone towards improvement.

One of the key aspects of embracing a growth mindset is the willingness to embrace failure and setbacks. Instead of letting failure define us, we learn from it and use it as a springboard for growth. This mindset encourages us to take risks, try new things, and step outside of our comfort zones. It enables us to constantly push ourselves to reach new heights and achieve breakthrough ideas.

Furthermore, cultivating a growth mindset fosters a love for learning. We become avid learners, seeking out new knowledge and skills to enhance our personal and professional lives. We understand that intelligence and abilities are not fixed, and therefore, we continuously strive to improve ourselves. This mindset allows us to adapt to changing circumstances and embrace new opportunities with enthusiasm.

In "The Innovator's Mind," we delve deep into the strategies and techniques for developing a growth mindset. We provide practical exercises and real-life examples to help you shift your perspective and embrace this powerful mindset. Whether you are a student, professional, or someone simply looking to enhance your mindset, this subchapter will provide you with the tools and insights you need to cultivate a growth mindset and unlock your full potential.

So, are you ready to embrace a growth mindset and embark on a journey of personal and professional growth? Join us in "The Innovator's Mind" as we explore the power of embracing this mindset and discover how it can lead to breakthrough ideas and greater success in all areas of life.

Overcoming Fear of Failure

Fear of failure is a common psychological barrier that holds many people back from reaching their full potential. Whether you are an entrepreneur, artist, or student, the fear of failure can hinder your creativity and prevent you from taking risks. However, by understanding and addressing this fear, you can cultivate a mindset of resilience and innovation.

In the subchapter "Overcoming Fear of Failure" from the book "The Innovator's Mind: Cultivating Creativity for Breakthrough Ideas," we explore the powerful techniques and strategies to conquer this fear and unleash your true potential. This chapter is addressed to anyone who wishes to break free from the shackles of fear and embrace a growth mindset.

We begin by delving into the psychology of fear and failure, exploring its origins and impact on our lives. Understanding that failure is an integral part of the learning process is crucial in overcoming this fear. We explore stories of successful individuals who have faced failure and how they managed to bounce back stronger than ever.

Next, we dive into practical techniques to reframe our mindset towards failure. By shifting our perspective, we can turn failure into an opportunity for growth and learning. We explore the concept of a growth mindset, popularized by psychologist Carol Dweck, and how it can transform our approach to failure.

Moreover, we delve into strategies to build resilience and overcome the fear of failure. From setting realistic goals to developing healthy coping mechanisms, we provide actionable steps to empower readers in their journey towards success.

Throughout the subchapter, we include thought-provoking exercises and reflections to help readers confront their fears and develop a resilient mindset. We also explore the concept of self-compassion and how it can counterbalance the fear of failure, fostering a supportive environment for personal growth.

By the end of this subchapter, readers will have gained valuable insights into overcoming the fear of failure and cultivating a growth mindset. They will be equipped with practical tools to embrace failure as a stepping stone towards innovation and breakthrough ideas.

"The Innovator's Mind: Cultivating Creativity for Breakthrough Ideas" offers a fresh perspective on success and provides readers with the necessary tools to unlock their creative potential. Through this subchapter on overcoming the fear of failure, readers will embark on a transformative journey towards a mindset of resilience, innovation, and success.

Cultivating Curiosity and Openness

In the pursuit of breakthrough ideas and creative thinking, one of the most important qualities to cultivate is curiosity. Curiosity is the fuel that drives innovation, propelling us to explore new possibilities, question assumptions, and seek out new knowledge. It is the spark that ignites our imagination and enables us to see beyond the status quo.

But how can we cultivate curiosity in our lives? How can we foster an environment that encourages open-mindedness and a thirst for learning? In this subchapter, we will explore the power of cultivating curiosity and openness, and how it can positively impact our mindset and success.

Curiosity is not just about being interested in new things; it's about actively seeking out new experiences and ideas. It involves having a genuine desire to learn, to understand, and to grow. By cultivating curiosity, we open ourselves up to new perspectives and possibilities, allowing us to see connections and patterns that others might miss.

To foster curiosity, it is important to create an environment that encourages exploration and questioning. This can be done by surrounding ourselves with diverse perspectives, engaging in thought-provoking conversations, and exposing ourselves to new experiences. By stepping out of our comfort zones and embracing the unknown, we open ourselves up to new ideas and opportunities for innovation.

Openness is another key component of cultivating an innovator's mindset. It involves having a willingness to consider different viewpoints, challenge our own beliefs, and embrace change. Openness allows us to approach problems with fresh eyes and to adapt to new circumstances. It is an essential quality for anyone seeking to make a meaningful impact in today's rapidly changing world.

To cultivate openness, it is important to practice active listening and empathy. By genuinely seeking to understand others' perspectives and experiences, we expand our own worldview and become more open to different ideas. Embracing diversity in all its forms – be it cultural, intellectual, or experiential – can also foster openness, as it exposes us to a wide range of perspectives and ways of thinking.

In conclusion, cultivating curiosity and openness is paramount for cultivating creativity and breakthrough ideas. By fostering a mindset of curiosity, we become lifelong learners, constantly seeking new knowledge and expanding our horizons. By embracing openness, we become adaptable and flexible, able to navigate the ever-changing landscape of innovation. Together, curiosity and openness form the foundation of the innovator's mind – a mind that is ready to explore, question, and create.

Nurturing a Positive Attitude towards Change

Change is an inevitable part of life. It can be exciting, challenging, and sometimes even daunting. However, those who embrace change with a positive attitude are more likely to thrive in today's fast-paced and dynamic world. In this subchapter, we will explore the importance of nurturing a positive attitude towards change and how it can cultivate creativity and lead to breakthrough ideas.

First and foremost, it is crucial to understand that change is a constant. Whether we like it or not, the world around us is continuously evolving. By embracing this reality, we can develop a mindset that sees change as an opportunity rather than a threat. This mindset shift sets the foundation for nurturing a positive attitude towards change.

To cultivate a positive attitude towards change, it is essential to develop resilience. Resilience allows us to bounce back from setbacks and adapt to new circumstances. One way to build resilience is by reframing challenges as learning opportunities. Instead of dwelling on the difficulties, we can focus on the growth and personal development that comes with navigating change.

Another key aspect of nurturing a positive attitude towards change is maintaining an open mind. An open mind allows us to explore new possibilities and consider alternative perspectives. By embracing different ideas and perspectives, we expand our creativity and increase our ability to generate breakthrough ideas. This openness to change is a fundamental trait of innovative thinkers.

Additionally, developing a growth mindset is crucial in fostering a positive attitude towards change. A growth mindset is the belief that our abilities and intelligence can be developed through dedication and hard work. With a growth mindset, we view challenges as opportunities to learn and improve, rather than as fixed limitations. This mindset empowers us to embrace change as a chance for personal and professional growth.

Lastly, it is essential to surround ourselves with a supportive network of like-minded individuals. A strong support system can provide encouragement, guidance, and reassurance during times of change. Collaborating with others who share a positive attitude towards change can fuel our creativity and inspire breakthrough ideas.

In conclusion, nurturing a positive attitude towards change is crucial for cultivating creativity and generating breakthrough ideas. By embracing change as an opportunity for growth, maintaining resilience, keeping an open mind, developing a growth mindset, and surrounding ourselves with a supportive network, we can foster a mindset that welcomes change and thrives in an ever-evolving world. So, let us embrace change and unleash our innovative potential.

Chapter 3: Unleashing Your Creative Potential

Tapping into Your Imagination

Imagination is a powerful tool that resides within each one of us. It is the driving force behind creativity and the key to unlocking breakthrough ideas. In this subchapter, we will explore the importance of tapping into your imagination and how it can cultivate creativity in your life.

Imagination is not just reserved for artists or writers; it is a skill that anyone can develop and harness. In fact, research has shown that individuals who tap into their imagination are more likely to succeed and find fulfillment in their endeavors. This is because imagination allows us to think outside the box, see possibilities where others see limitations, and come up with innovative solutions to problems.

To tap into your imagination, it is essential to adopt a growth mindset. The concept of mindset, as popularized by psychologist Carol Dweck in her book "Mindset: The New Psychology of Success," suggests that our beliefs about our abilities can either limit or enhance our potential. By adopting a growth mindset, you believe that your intelligence, talents, and abilities can be developed through dedication and hard work. This mindset allows you to embrace challenges, learn from failure, and ultimately tap into your imagination.

One practical way to tap into your imagination is through visualization exercises. Take a few moments each day to close your eyes and imagine yourself in different scenarios. Picture yourself in a place you've never been, doing something you've never done. Allow your mind to wander freely and explore new possibilities. This exercise strengthens your imaginative muscles and expands your capacity for creative thinking.

Another way to tap into your imagination is through exposure to new experiences and ideas. Seek out new perspectives, explore different cultures, and engage in activities outside of your comfort zone. This exposure helps you break free from your mental constraints and allows your imagination to soar.

Furthermore, surrounding yourself with like-minded individuals who encourage and support your imaginative pursuits can have a profound impact on your creativity. Join communities, attend workshops, or find a mentor who shares your passion for innovation. Collaborating with others who are also tapping into their imagination can spark new ideas and inspire you to think even more creatively.

In conclusion, tapping into your imagination is crucial for cultivating creativity and generating breakthrough ideas. By adopting a growth mindset, practicing visualization exercises, exposing yourself to new experiences, and connecting with like-minded individuals, you can unlock the full potential of your imagination. So, embrace the power of your mind, and let your imagination take you on a journey of limitless possibilities.

Developing Critical Thinking Skills

In the fast-paced and ever-changing world we live in, the ability to think critically has become a crucial skill for success. Whether you are a student, professional, or simply seeking personal growth, developing your critical thinking skills is essential for navigating through life's challenges and making informed decisions. In this subchapter, we will explore the importance of developing critical thinking skills and provide practical guidance on how to cultivate this valuable trait.

Critical thinking is the process of objectively analyzing and evaluating information, ideas, and arguments. It goes beyond just accepting what we are told or relying on our intuition. It involves questioning assumptions, considering different perspectives, and drawing logical conclusions based on evidence. By strengthening our critical thinking skills, we become better equipped to solve problems, make sound judgments, and generate innovative ideas.

One key aspect of developing critical thinking skills is adopting a growth mindset. As discussed in the book "Mindset: The New Psychology of Success," a growth mindset is the belief that our abilities and intelligence can be developed through dedication and hard work. By embracing this mindset, we open ourselves up to new possibilities and are more willing to engage in critical thinking. We understand that intelligence is not fixed, and we can always improve our thinking abilities.

To develop critical thinking skills, it is important to engage in activities that challenge our minds. Reading thought-provoking books, engaging in debates, and solving complex problems are all effective ways to sharpen our thinking abilities. Additionally, seeking out diverse perspectives and actively listening to others' opinions can help us broaden our understanding and think more critically.

Another valuable tool in developing critical thinking skills is reflection. Taking the time to reflect on our own thoughts, actions, and beliefs allows us to analyze them objectively and identify potential biases or logical fallacies. Journaling or engaging in regular self-reflection exercises can help us become more self-aware and improve our critical thinking abilities.

In conclusion, developing critical thinking skills is imperative in today's rapidly changing world. By adopting a growth mindset and engaging in challenging activities, we can enhance our ability to think critically and make better decisions. Remember, critical thinking is not a fixed trait but a skill that can be developed and honed over time. So, let's embrace the journey of cultivating our critical thinking skills and unlock our full potential for creativity and breakthrough ideas.

Enhancing Problem-Solving Abilities

In today's rapidly changing world, problem-solving abilities have become an essential skill for success in any field. Whether you are an entrepreneur, a student, or a professional, the ability to effectively solve problems can help you navigate challenges, seize opportunities, and achieve breakthrough ideas. This subchapter explores various strategies and techniques to enhance your problem-solving abilities, drawing inspiration from the principles of the book, "The Innovator's Mind: Cultivating Creativity for Breakthrough Ideas" and the concept of mindset discussed in "Mindset: The New Psychology of Success."

1. Embrace a Growth Mindset: Developing a growth mindset is crucial for enhancing problem-solving abilities. Understand that intelligence and abilities are not fixed traits, but can be improved through effort and learning. Embrace challenges, view setbacks as opportunities for growth, and persist in the face of obstacles. By believing in your ability to learn and improve, you can approach problem-solving with an open mind and a willingness to explore new ideas.

2. Think Outside the Box: To find innovative solutions, it is important to break free from conventional thinking patterns. Challenge assumptions, question existing norms, and explore alternative perspectives. Adopt a sense of curiosity and explore diverse sources of inspiration. By broadening your horizons and thinking creatively, you can uncover unique and unexpected solutions to complex problems.

3. Collaborate and Seek Feedback: Problem-solving is not a solitary endeavor. Engage in collaborative problem-solving by seeking input from diverse perspectives. Embrace teamwork and leverage the collective intelligence of a group. Actively listen to others' ideas, encourage open dialogue, and create an environment where everyone

feels comfortable sharing their thoughts. Additionally, seek feedback from mentors, peers, or experts to gain valuable insights and refine your problem-solving approach.

4. Break Down Problems: Complex problems can often feel overwhelming. Break them down into smaller, more manageable components. This allows you to focus on one aspect at a time, identify root causes, and generate targeted solutions. By systematically deconstructing problems, you can gain a better understanding of the underlying issues and develop effective strategies to address them.

5. Iterate and Learn from Failures: Problem-solving is an iterative process. Embrace a mindset of continuous improvement and learn from failures along the way. Treat setbacks as learning opportunities and analyze the reasons behind them. Adjust your approach, experiment with different solutions, and refine your strategies based on feedback and results. By embracing a growth mindset and learning from each experience, you can enhance your problem-solving abilities over time.

In conclusion, enhancing problem-solving abilities is crucial for success in today's fast-paced world. By embracing a growth mindset, thinking creatively, collaborating with others, breaking down problems, and learning from failures, you can cultivate your problem-solving skills and unlock breakthrough ideas. Adopting these strategies from "The Innovator's Mind: Cultivating Creativity for Breakthrough Ideas" and the principles of mindset from "Mindset: The New Psychology of Success" can empower you to tackle challenges head-on, find innovative solutions, and thrive in any endeavor.

Stimulating Divergent Thinking

In the quest for breakthrough ideas, one essential skill stands out: divergent thinking. This is the ability to generate multiple solutions, perspectives, and possibilities to a given problem or challenge. Engaging in divergent thinking not only expands our creativity but also enhances our problem-solving abilities. In this subchapter, we will explore various strategies and techniques to stimulate divergent thinking and cultivate an innovative mindset.

1. Embrace Curiosity: Curiosity is the fuel that drives divergent thinking. By cultivating a curious mindset, we can explore new ideas, ask thought-provoking questions, and challenge conventional wisdom. We must encourage ourselves to be open-minded and inquisitive, constantly seeking new knowledge and experiences.

2. Encourage Brainstorming Sessions: Brainstorming sessions are a classic tool for stimulating divergent thinking. The key is to create a safe and non-judgmental environment where all ideas are welcomed. Encourage participants to think outside the box, challenge assumptions, and build upon each other's ideas. Remember, the goal is quantity over quality at this stage.

3. Incorporate Mind Mapping: Mind mapping is a visual technique that helps organize thoughts and connections around a central idea. This approach encourages divergent thinking by allowing us to explore various branches and possibilities emanating from a single concept. It helps us see relationships, spark new ideas, and identify potential solutions.

4. Seek Diverse Perspectives: Divergent thinking thrives on diverse perspectives. Surround yourself with people from different

backgrounds, cultures, and industries. Engage in conversations, attend conferences, and seek out diverse opinions. By exposing ourselves to different viewpoints, we can challenge our own assumptions and tap into a broader range of ideas.

5. Practice Reverse Thinking: Reverse thinking involves challenging the conventional approach to a problem and considering the opposite perspective. By exploring the opposite direction, we can uncover new possibilities and innovative solutions. This technique forces us to break free from our comfort zones and consider alternative perspectives.

6. Embrace Failure as a Learning Opportunity: Divergent thinking requires us to take risks and embrace failure as a natural part of the creative process. Failure provides valuable feedback and helps us refine our ideas. By reframing failure as a learning opportunity, we can overcome fear and unleash our creative potential.

Stimulating divergent thinking is a crucial step towards cultivating an innovative mindset. By embracing curiosity, incorporating brainstorming sessions, utilizing mind mapping techniques, seeking diverse perspectives, practicing reverse thinking, and embracing failure, we can expand our creative boundaries and unlock breakthrough ideas. Remember, divergent thinking is not just reserved for the select few; it is a skill that anyone can develop with practice and perseverance.

Chapter 4: Cultivating Creativity in Everyday Life

Creating a Supportive Environment

In the pursuit of breakthrough ideas and cultivating creativity, creating a supportive environment plays a crucial role. The environment we surround ourselves with greatly influences our mindset, motivation, and ultimately, our success. In this subchapter, we will explore the importance of creating a supportive environment and how it can enhance our ability to innovate and generate breakthrough ideas.

Our mindset, as highlighted in the book "Mindset: The New Psychology of Success," is a fundamental factor that determines our approach to challenges and opportunities. A supportive environment helps us develop a growth mindset, where we embrace challenges, persist through setbacks, and view failures as learning opportunities. When we are surrounded by individuals who share this mindset, we are more likely to take risks and explore new possibilities without fear of judgment or criticism.

One aspect of creating a supportive environment is fostering a culture of collaboration and open communication. When we have access to diverse perspectives and ideas, our own thinking expands, and we become more open to innovation. Encouraging brainstorming sessions and group discussions can provide a platform for individuals to share their thoughts and bounce ideas off one another. This collaborative environment not only generates a constant flow of fresh ideas but also fosters a sense of belonging and collective motivation.

Another crucial aspect of a supportive environment is providing the necessary resources and infrastructure for individuals to thrive. This may include access to tools, technologies, and information that stimulate creativity and innovation. When individuals have the necessary resources at their disposal, they are more likely to experiment, explore, and take risks in their pursuit of breakthrough ideas.

Furthermore, a supportive environment should also prioritize the well-being and personal growth of individuals. This can be achieved through mentorship programs, training sessions, and opportunities for professional development. When individuals feel supported in their personal and professional growth, they are more likely to take on challenges and push their creative boundaries.

In conclusion, creating a supportive environment is crucial for cultivating creativity and generating breakthrough ideas. By fostering a growth mindset, encouraging collaboration, providing necessary resources, and prioritizing personal growth, individuals can thrive in an environment that nurtures their creativity and innovation. Whether you are an entrepreneur, an artist, or anyone seeking to unleash their creative potential, understanding the significance of a supportive environment is essential on the path to success.

Practicing Mindfulness and Reflection

In today's fast-paced and ever-changing world, cultivating mindfulness and reflection has become more important than ever. In the book "The Innovator's Mind: Cultivating Creativity for Breakthrough Ideas," we delve into the significance of these practices and how they can contribute to personal growth, success, and creativity.

Mindfulness, often associated with meditation and being present in the moment, has gained popularity in recent years for its ability to reduce stress and enhance overall well-being. However, its benefits extend far beyond that. By training our minds to be fully present and aware, we can tap into our true potential and unleash our creativity.

In the chapter on Practicing Mindfulness and Reflection, we explore various techniques and exercises to develop mindfulness. We delve into the power of observing our thoughts and emotions without judgment, learning to let go of distractions, and cultivating a sense of curiosity and openness. Through these practices, individuals can develop a deeper understanding of themselves, their thoughts, and their emotions, leading to enhanced self-awareness and personal growth.

Reflection, on the other hand, involves taking the time to contemplate and evaluate our experiences, actions, and decisions. It allows us to make sense of our thoughts and emotions and gain valuable insights that can guide our future actions. Reflection is not about dwelling on the past or ruminating on mistakes but rather about learning from our experiences and using that knowledge to make better choices moving forward.

In "The Innovator's Mind," we provide practical tips and exercises for incorporating reflection into your daily routine. Whether it's through journaling, engaging in meaningful conversations, or setting aside dedicated time for self-reflection, these practices can help you gain clarity, make more informed decisions, and ultimately foster breakthrough ideas.

By combining mindfulness and reflection, individuals can cultivate a growth mindset, a concept explored in "Mindset: The New Psychology of Success." This mindset is characterized by a belief in the power of effort, learning, and resilience. It allows individuals to view challenges as opportunities for growth and embrace failure as a stepping stone towards success.

In conclusion, practicing mindfulness and reflection can have a profound impact on our personal and professional lives. By incorporating these practices into our daily routines, we can develop a deeper understanding of ourselves, enhance our creativity, and cultivate a growth mindset. "The Innovator's Mind" offers valuable insights and practical strategies to help anyone harness the power of mindfulness and reflection on their journey towards personal and professional success.

Seeking Inspiration from Different Sources

In the pursuit of creativity and breakthrough ideas, seeking inspiration from different sources is a powerful tool that can enhance our thought processes and ignite innovation. The ability to draw inspiration from a variety of disciplines and perspectives is what separates true innovators from the rest. In this subchapter, we will explore the significance of seeking inspiration from different sources and how it can cultivate an innovator's mind.

The first step towards seeking inspiration is to broaden our horizons and embrace diverse experiences. By immersing ourselves in different cultures, exploring new places, and engaging with people from various backgrounds, we expose ourselves to different perspectives and ways of thinking. This exposure helps us see the world through a different lens, opening our minds to new ideas and possibilities.

Another way to seek inspiration is by exploring various art forms. Whether it's visual arts, music, literature, or even performance arts, each art form has the potential to spark our imagination and trigger new thoughts. By observing and appreciating the creativity of others, we can tap into our own creative reservoir and develop unique ideas.

Science and technology are also great sources of inspiration. The constant advancements in these fields provide us with a wealth of knowledge and ideas that can be applied to different domains. By staying updated with the latest research and breakthroughs, we can integrate scientific principles into our own work, pushing the boundaries of innovation even further.

Nature, too, can offer a profound source of inspiration. The intricate designs found in the natural world, from the patterns on butterfly wings to the structure of a snowflake, can serve as a reminder of the limitless possibilities that exist. Observing nature's beauty can inspire us to think outside the box and apply its principles to our own creative endeavors.

Lastly, seeking inspiration from people who have achieved greatness can be incredibly powerful. Learning about the journeys and accomplishments of individuals who have made significant contributions in their respective fields can motivate us to strive for excellence. Their stories can provide valuable insights and serve as a reminder that breakthrough ideas are within reach.

In conclusion, seeking inspiration from different sources is essential for cultivating an innovator's mind. By embracing diverse experiences, exploring various art forms, staying updated with scientific advancements, connecting with nature, and learning from great individuals, we can expand our creative thinking and unlock breakthrough ideas. As we continue our journey towards cultivating creativity, let us remember to seek inspiration from the world around us and embrace the power of diverse perspectives.

Experimenting and Taking Risks

In today's fast-paced and ever-changing world, it is essential to possess the ability to adapt, innovate, and think outside the box. This is especially true when it comes to cultivating creativity and generating breakthrough ideas. In the subchapter "Experimenting and Taking Risks" of the book "The Innovator's Mind: Cultivating Creativity for Breakthrough Ideas," we delve into the importance of embracing experimentation and taking risks in order to foster a mindset of success.

Experimentation is the cornerstone of innovation. It involves stepping outside of our comfort zones and exploring uncharted territories. By experimenting, we open ourselves up to new possibilities and allow ourselves to view problems from different angles. This mindset shift enables us to break free from conventional thinking and discover groundbreaking solutions.

However, experimentation alone is not enough. It must be coupled with the willingness to take risks. Taking risks involves embracing uncertainty and being open to failure. Often, our fear of failure hinders our ability to take the necessary risks for innovation. But it is through these failures that we learn and grow. Every failure brings us closer to success by providing valuable insights and lessons that help us refine our ideas.

To cultivate a mindset of experimentation and risk-taking, we must overcome our fear of failure and embrace a growth mindset. In Carol S. Dweck's book "Mindset: The New Psychology of Success," she explores the power of adopting a growth mindset, where failures are seen as opportunities for growth rather than setbacks. By shifting our perspective and viewing failure as a stepping stone towards success, we become more resilient and better equipped to overcome obstacles.

Moreover, embracing experimentation and taking risks requires an environment that supports and encourages these behaviors. Creating a safe space where failure is not stigmatized but celebrated as a necessary part of the innovation process is crucial. This fosters a culture of curiosity, collaboration, and continuous learning, where individuals feel empowered to share their ideas and take calculated risks without the fear of judgment.

In conclusion, the subchapter "Experimenting and Taking Risks" explores the pivotal role of experimentation and risk-taking in cultivating an innovative mindset. By embracing experimentation, taking risks, and adopting a growth mindset, we unlock our potential for breakthrough ideas and pave the way for success. It is through these bold steps that we can truly cultivate creativity and make a lasting impact in a world that is constantly evolving.

Chapter 5: The Creative Process: From Ideation to Implementation

Defining the Stages of the Creative Process

Creativity is a powerful force that drives innovation, and understanding the stages of the creative process is essential for harnessing this force effectively. In this subchapter, we will explore the various stages of the creative process and how they contribute to cultivating breakthrough ideas. Whether you are an entrepreneur, artist, or simply someone looking to enhance their problem-solving skills, understanding these stages will empower you to tap into your creative potential.

The first stage of the creative process is preparation. This stage involves gathering information, exploring ideas, and immersing oneself in the subject matter. It is during this stage that the mind begins to form connections and identify patterns, setting the foundation for the creative journey ahead. Preparation involves research, brainstorming, and seeking inspiration from various sources. By expanding our knowledge and understanding, we create a fertile ground for creative ideas to take root.

The second stage is incubation. After the preparation stage, it is important to step back and allow the mind to process the gathered information. This stage may involve taking a break, engaging in unrelated activities, or simply giving oneself time to reflect. Incubation allows the subconscious mind to work its magic, making unexpected connections and generating new insights. It is during this stage that breakthrough ideas often emerge seemingly out of nowhere.

The next stage is illumination. This is the "aha" moment when the creative solution becomes clear. It is a sudden burst of insight or understanding that brings the pieces of the puzzle together. Illumination can happen at any time and often when least expected. It is crucial to embrace and capture these moments by recording ideas or sketching them out. Without proper documentation, these fleeting moments of brilliance can easily slip away.

The final stage of the creative process is verification. This stage involves evaluating and refining the ideas generated during the illumination stage. It is a critical step where ideas are tested, analyzed, and developed further. Verification requires feedback, experimentation, and iteration. By refining and polishing our ideas, we increase their chances of success and ensure they align with our intended goals.

Understanding and embracing the stages of the creative process is vital for cultivating innovation and breakthrough ideas. By recognizing the importance of preparation, incubation, illumination, and verification, we can tap into our creative potential and unlock new possibilities. Whether you are a seasoned innovator or someone looking to enhance your problem-solving skills, mastering the creative process will empower you to think outside the box and make a lasting impact in your chosen field.

Generating and Evaluating Ideas

Ideas are the lifeblood of innovation. They have the power to transform our world and shape the future. In this subchapter, we will explore the process of generating and evaluating ideas, providing you with the tools and techniques to cultivate creativity and unleash your potential for breakthrough ideas.

The first step in generating ideas is to create an environment that fosters creativity. This includes cultivating a growth mindset, as outlined in the book "Mindset: The New Psychology of Success." A growth mindset is the belief that abilities and intelligence can be developed through dedication and hard work. By adopting this mindset, you open yourself up to new possibilities and embrace challenges as opportunities for growth.

Once you have established the right mindset, it is time to embark on the journey of ideation. There are several techniques that can help you generate ideas. One such technique is brainstorming, where you gather a group of diverse individuals and encourage them to freely share their thoughts and suggestions. This allows for the cross-pollination of ideas and often leads to unexpected and innovative solutions.

Another technique is mind mapping. This involves creating a visual representation of your thoughts and ideas, allowing you to see connections and patterns that may not be immediately apparent. By mapping out your ideas, you can unlock new insights and perspectives.

However, generating ideas is only the first step. The next crucial step is evaluating and selecting the most promising ideas. To do this effectively, you need to develop a framework for evaluation. This framework should consider factors such as feasibility, market potential, and alignment with your goals and values.

One technique that can aid in the evaluation process is the SWOT analysis. SWOT stands for strengths, weaknesses, opportunities, and threats. By systematically analyzing these factors, you can gain a comprehensive understanding of each idea's potential and make informed decisions.

It is also important to seek feedback from others during the evaluation process. By sharing your ideas with trusted individuals, you can gain valuable insights and perspectives that can help refine and improve your concepts.

Remember, generating and evaluating ideas is an iterative process. It requires persistence, open-mindedness, and a willingness to embrace failure as a stepping stone to success. By cultivating a mindset of creativity and employing effective ideation techniques, you can unlock your innovative potential and cultivate breakthrough ideas that have the power to change the world.

Refining and Prototyping Concepts

In the ever-evolving landscape of innovation and creativity, one of the crucial steps towards achieving breakthrough ideas is refining and prototyping concepts. This subchapter explores the importance of this process and provides valuable insights into how to cultivate a mindset that fosters success in refining and prototyping.

To begin with, refining concepts is an essential step in the creative process. It involves carefully analyzing and evaluating ideas to enhance their feasibility, viability, and desirability. Refining allows us to take a critical look at our initial concepts, identifying areas that need improvement or modification. It is through this iterative process that we can transform raw ideas into refined concepts that are more likely to succeed in the real world.

Prototyping, on the other hand, is the tangible manifestation of refined concepts. It involves creating a working model or a minimum viable product (MVP) to test and validate the core ideas. Prototyping allows us to gather valuable feedback, identify potential flaws, and make necessary adjustments before investing significant resources into full-scale implementation. It is a crucial step in reducing risks and increasing the chances of success.

In cultivating a mindset that embraces the refining and prototyping process, it is essential to adopt a growth mindset. As discussed in the groundbreaking book "Mindset: The New Psychology of Success," by Carol S. Dweck, a growth mindset is the belief that our abilities and intelligence can be developed through dedication and hard work. By adopting a growth mindset, we understand that refining and prototyping are not simply about finding flaws but rather opportunities for improvement and learning.

Another key aspect of refining and prototyping concepts is maintaining a sense of curiosity and openness to feedback. Embracing feedback, both positive and negative, allows us to gain valuable insights and perspectives that can help refine our concepts further. It is through this continuous learning process that breakthrough ideas can emerge.

Furthermore, it is crucial to create an environment that encourages experimentation and risk-taking. By embracing failure as a stepping stone to success, we can overcome the fear of making mistakes and explore new possibilities. This mindset shift enables us to refine our concepts fearlessly and prototype them with confidence.

In conclusion, refining and prototyping concepts are essential steps in the creative process. By cultivating a growth mindset, embracing feedback, and fostering a culture of experimentation, we can refine our ideas and transform them into breakthrough innovations. So, let us embark on this journey of refining and prototyping, armed with the understanding that every iteration brings us closer to realizing our creative potential.

Implementing and Iterating on Innovative Solutions

Innovation is the lifeblood of progress and success in any field, industry, or endeavor. However, generating breakthrough ideas is just the first step. In order to truly revolutionize and make a lasting impact, these ideas must be implemented and iterated upon. This subchapter will delve into the crucial process of bringing innovative solutions to life and the mindset required for success.

Implementing an innovative solution is often a complex and multifaceted process. It requires a deep understanding of the problem being addressed, the resources available, and the potential obstacles that may arise. One must also consider the various stakeholders involved and ensure their buy-in and support. This calls for effective communication, collaboration, and leadership skills. An innovator must be able to inspire and motivate others, while also being open to feedback and ideas from all sources.

Iterating on innovative solutions is equally important. Rarely does the first iteration of an idea result in perfection. Through continuous improvement, refinement, and adaptation, an innovator can enhance their solution and increase its impact. This requires a growth mindset, one that embraces failure as a learning opportunity and sees setbacks as stepping stones towards success. By iterating on their ideas, innovators can stay ahead of the curve and adapt to changing circumstances and needs.

To implement and iterate on innovative solutions, one must cultivate certain habits and practices. First and foremost, it is essential to foster a culture of experimentation and risk-taking. This means creating an environment where failure is not only accepted but encouraged. It also requires the ability to think outside the box and challenge conventional wisdom. Innovators must be willing to question the status quo and explore new possibilities.

Additionally, effective implementation and iteration require a focus on data and feedback. By collecting and analyzing data, innovators can gain valuable insights into the effectiveness of their solutions and make informed decisions. Feedback from users, customers, and other stakeholders is also crucial in identifying areas for improvement and discovering unmet needs.

In conclusion, implementing and iterating on innovative solutions is a vital process in the pursuit of breakthrough ideas. It requires a mindset that embraces experimentation, failure, and continuous improvement. By fostering a culture of innovation, embracing feedback, and using data to inform decisions, innovators can bring their ideas to life and create lasting impact in their respective fields.

Chapter 6: Collaboration and Creativity: Fueling Breakthrough Ideas

The Power of Collaboration in Innovation

Innovation has long been considered a solitary pursuit, with the image of the lone genius tirelessly working in their laboratory to create groundbreaking ideas. However, in today's interconnected and rapidly changing world, the power of collaboration in innovation cannot be underestimated. The era of the lone genius is over, and the future belongs to those who can harness the collective intelligence and diverse perspectives of a group.

Collaboration is essential in the innovation process because it brings together individuals with different backgrounds, experiences, and expertise. By working together, they can combine their unique knowledge and skills, sparking new ideas and pushing the boundaries of what is possible. When people collaborate, they can build upon each other's ideas, challenge assumptions, and generate innovative solutions that no individual could have come up with on their own.

Moreover, collaboration fosters a culture of creativity and openness. When people feel supported and encouraged to share their ideas, they are more likely to take risks, think outside the box, and explore unconventional approaches. Collaboration also encourages active listening and empathy, allowing team members to understand and appreciate diverse perspectives. This leads to richer debates, deeper insights, and ultimately, more robust and innovative solutions.

Collaboration also plays a crucial role in overcoming the challenges that innovation often presents. Innovating requires experimentation, and not all ideas will be successful. However, by collaborating, teams can leverage the collective wisdom to quickly identify and learn from failures, iterate, and pivot towards more promising paths. Collaboration also enables teams to pool resources, share expertise, and leverage networks, increasing the likelihood of successfully bringing innovative ideas to fruition.

To truly harness the power of collaboration in innovation, a shift in mindset is necessary. Gone are the days of guarding ideas jealously and working in isolation. Instead, individuals and organizations must embrace a culture of collaboration, where sharing knowledge, building on each other's ideas, and fostering a sense of collective ownership are valued. This requires letting go of ego, being open to feedback, and embracing diversity.

In conclusion, collaboration is the key to unlocking innovation in the modern world. By bringing together diverse perspectives, fostering a culture of creativity and openness, and overcoming challenges through collective wisdom, collaboration enables breakthrough ideas and drives success. Embracing the power of collaboration is not only beneficial for individuals and organizations but also for society as a whole, as it paves the way for groundbreaking solutions to the complex challenges we face in the 21st century.

Building and Leading Creative Teams

In today's rapidly changing world, creativity and innovation have become essential for success in any field. Whether you are an entrepreneur, a manager, or an employee, having a team that can think creatively and generate breakthrough ideas is crucial. This subchapter, titled "Building and Leading Creative Teams," from the book "The Innovator's Mind: Cultivating Creativity for Breakthrough Ideas," explores the mindset and strategies necessary to foster creativity within teams and lead them towards innovative solutions.

One of the key aspects of building a creative team is fostering a growth mindset. According to the research in "Mindset: The New Psychology of Success," individuals who believe in their ability to develop their skills and intelligence are more likely to embrace challenges and persevere through obstacles. As a leader, it is important to cultivate this mindset within your team members, encouraging them to take risks and view failures as learning opportunities.

Furthermore, creating a diverse and inclusive team is essential for generating innovative ideas. Different perspectives and backgrounds bring unique insights and approaches to problem-solving. The book emphasizes the importance of embracing diversity and creating an environment where everyone feels valued and included. This can be achieved through open communication, active listening, and fostering a culture of respect and collaboration.

In addition to mindset and diversity, the subchapter delves into practical strategies for promoting creativity within teams. It explores techniques such as brainstorming, ideation sessions, and design thinking. These methods encourage team members to think outside the box, challenge assumptions, and explore unconventional solutions.

Moreover, the subchapter provides guidance on effective leadership techniques to inspire and guide creative teams. It explores the concept of servant leadership, where leaders prioritize the needs of their team members and empower them to take ownership of their work. It also emphasizes the importance of providing a safe and supportive environment where individuals feel comfortable expressing their ideas and taking risks.

Overall, "Building and Leading Creative Teams" is a subchapter that offers practical insights and strategies for cultivating a creative mindset within teams and leading them towards breakthrough ideas. It addresses the audience of "anyone" who is interested in fostering creativity and innovation in their respective fields. By implementing the principles and techniques outlined in this subchapter, individuals can create an environment where creativity flourishes, leading to greater success and innovation.

Fostering a Culture of Collaboration

In today's rapidly changing world, collaboration has become a key driver of success. No longer can individuals or organizations thrive in isolation. Instead, a culture of collaboration has emerged as the new norm, fueling innovation and breakthrough ideas. In this subchapter, we will explore the importance of fostering such a culture and provide practical strategies for cultivating collaboration within any organization or team.

At its core, collaboration is about bringing diverse perspectives together to solve complex problems and generate innovative solutions. It is a mindset that recognizes the power of collective intelligence and the value of shared knowledge. By fostering a culture of collaboration, individuals and teams can tap into this collective wisdom, creating a dynamic environment that nurtures creativity and fosters breakthrough ideas.

One of the key elements in fostering a culture of collaboration is creating an environment that celebrates and encourages teamwork. This can be achieved by promoting open communication, creating spaces for collaboration, and recognizing and rewarding collaborative efforts. When individuals feel supported and valued for their contributions as part of a team, they are more likely to actively engage in collaborative endeavors.

Another important aspect is building trust among team members. Trust is the foundation upon which effective collaboration is built. By fostering an environment of trust, where individuals feel safe to share their ideas, take risks, and challenge the status quo, teams can foster open and honest communication, leading to deeper collaboration and innovation.

Furthermore, leaders play a crucial role in fostering a culture of collaboration. They must lead by example, demonstrating the value of collaboration through their actions and behaviors. By encouraging cross-functional collaboration, breaking down silos, and providing resources and support, leaders can empower individuals to work together towards a common goal.

In conclusion, fostering a culture of collaboration is essential for cultivating creativity and generating breakthrough ideas. By embracing collaboration as a mindset and implementing strategies that promote teamwork, trust, and leadership support, any organization or team can create an environment where innovation thrives. So, let us embrace the power of collaboration and unlock the potential for transformative ideas that can shape our future.

Leveraging Diversity for Creative Problem-Solving

In today's rapidly changing world, creativity and innovation have become crucial for success in any field. To cultivate breakthrough ideas, individuals and organizations must embrace diversity and harness its power to enhance problem-solving. In this subchapter of "The Innovator's Mind: Cultivating Creativity for Breakthrough Ideas," we will explore how leveraging diversity can lead to more innovative and effective problem-solving strategies.

Diversity can take many forms, including cultural, gender, age, and cognitive differences. By bringing together individuals with diverse backgrounds and perspectives, teams can tap into a wealth of ideas and insights that can drive creative problem-solving. Research has consistently shown that diverse teams outperform homogeneous ones in generating new ideas and solving complex problems. This is because diverse teams offer a wider range of perspectives, experiences, and knowledge, enabling them to approach problems from different angles and come up with unique solutions.

One of the key benefits of leveraging diversity for creative problem-solving is the ability to overcome cognitive biases. When individuals from different backgrounds collaborate, they challenge each other's assumptions and biases, leading to more balanced and well-rounded decision-making. This can help teams avoid groupthink and foster a culture of open-mindedness where everyone feels comfortable expressing their ideas.

Another advantage of diversity in problem-solving is the ability to tap into collective intelligence. By combining different perspectives and insights, teams can leverage the collective knowledge and expertise of their members, leading to more robust solutions. This can result in breakthrough ideas that would have been impossible to achieve by individuals working in isolation.

However, leveraging diversity for creative problem-solving also requires creating an inclusive and supportive environment. It is not enough to simply have a diverse team; individuals must feel valued and respected for their unique contributions. Leaders should promote a culture of inclusivity, where everyone's voice is heard and diverse perspectives are actively sought out. By fostering an environment that celebrates diversity, organizations can unlock the full potential of their teams and drive innovation.

In conclusion, diversity is a powerful tool for enhancing creative problem-solving. By leveraging the unique perspectives, experiences, and knowledge of diverse individuals, teams can generate breakthrough ideas and find innovative solutions. However, it is essential to create an inclusive environment that values and respects diversity to fully harness its potential. By embracing diversity and cultivating a mindset that embraces different perspectives, individuals and organizations can unlock their creative potential and thrive in today's fast-paced and ever-changing world.

Chapter 7: Overcoming Blocks to Creativity

Identifying and Addressing Creative Blocks

In the fast-paced and ever-evolving world we live in, creativity has become a highly sought-after skill. Whether you're an artist, a scientist, an entrepreneur, or simply someone who wants to think outside the box, cultivating creativity is essential for generating breakthrough ideas. However, even the most innovative minds can sometimes find themselves facing creative blocks – those frustrating moments when ideas seem to dry up, inspiration wanes, and progress stalls. In this subchapter, we will explore the common causes of creative blocks and provide practical strategies for overcoming them.

One of the first steps in addressing creative blocks is recognizing their origins. Often, these blocks are rooted in fear – fear of failure, fear of judgment, or fear of the unknown. By acknowledging and understanding these fears, we can begin to dismantle the mental barriers that hinder our creative thinking. Cultivating a growth mindset, as outlined in Carol Dweck's book "Mindset: The New Psychology of Success," is a powerful tool for overcoming these fears. Embracing the belief that our abilities can be developed through dedication and hard work allows us to view setbacks as opportunities for growth rather than indications of our limitations.

Another common cause of creative blocks is burnout. In our fast-paced society, it's easy to become overwhelmed and exhausted, leaving little room for creative thinking. Recognizing the importance of self-care and creating a balanced lifestyle is crucial for nurturing our creativity. Taking breaks, engaging in physical activities, and finding time for hobbies and interests outside of work can help replenish our mental energy and stimulate fresh ideas.

Moreover, the environment we surround ourselves with can either foster or impede creativity. Cluttered workspaces, distractions, and a lack of inspiration can all contribute to creative blocks. Creating an environment that promotes focus and inspiration is essential. This may involve decluttering our physical spaces, incorporating elements that inspire us, or finding alternative work locations that stimulate our creativity.

Lastly, seeking external input and collaborating with others can help overcome creative blocks. Engaging in discussions, brainstorming sessions, or seeking feedback from trusted peers can provide fresh perspectives and new ideas. Sometimes, simply bouncing ideas off someone else can help break through mental roadblocks and spark creativity.

In conclusion, creative blocks are a natural part of the creative process, but they don't have to be permanent. By identifying the causes of these blocks and applying practical strategies, such as embracing a growth mindset, practicing self-care, creating an inspiring environment, and seeking external input, we can effectively address and overcome creative blocks. By cultivating our creativity, we enhance our ability to generate breakthrough ideas and become true innovators in our respective fields.

Managing Self-Doubt and Criticism

Self-doubt and criticism are common obstacles that can hinder our creativity and prevent us from reaching our full potential. In this subchapter of "The Innovator's Mind: Cultivating Creativity for

Breakthrough Ideas," we will explore strategies and techniques to effectively manage self-doubt and criticism, allowing us to develop a resilient mindset and unleash our creative abilities.

Self-doubt often arises from our fear of failure or feeling inadequate compared to others. However, it is important to acknowledge that self-doubt is a natural part of the creative process. Recognizing and accepting this fact can help us reframe self-doubt as an opportunity for growth and learning. By adopting a growth mindset, as described in "Mindset: The New Psychology of Success," we can view challenges and setbacks as stepping stones towards improvement rather than as indicators of our worth.

One way to manage self-doubt is by cultivating self-compassion. Instead of being overly critical of ourselves, we can practice being kind and understanding, just as we would with a close friend. By acknowledging our strengths and celebrating our accomplishments, we can build self-confidence and counteract self-doubt.

Criticism can also be a significant deterrent to our creativity. However, it is important to differentiate between constructive criticism and destructive criticism. Constructive criticism, when given with good intentions, can provide valuable insights and help us refine our ideas. On the other hand, destructive criticism is often fueled by personal agendas or negativity and should be disregarded.

To effectively manage criticism, it is crucial to remain open-minded and receptive. Instead of immediately dismissing criticism, take a step back and objectively evaluate its validity. By considering different perspectives, we can gain a deeper understanding of our work and make necessary improvements. In addition, seeking feedback from trusted mentors or peers can provide valuable guidance and support.

Developing a strong support network is another crucial aspect of managing self-doubt and criticism. Surrounding ourselves with like-minded individuals who understand and encourage our creative pursuits can provide the motivation and reassurance we need to overcome self-doubt. Sharing our experiences and challenges with others can also help us realize that self-doubt and criticism are universal and not exclusive to our own journey.

In conclusion, managing self-doubt and criticism is essential for cultivating creativity and achieving breakthrough ideas. By adopting a growth mindset, practicing self-compassion, differentiating between constructive and destructive criticism, remaining open-minded, and building a support network, we can effectively navigate these challenges and harness our full creative potential. Remember, self-doubt and criticism are not roadblocks but rather opportunities for growth and self-improvement.

Dealing with Perfectionism

Perfectionism can be both a blessing and a curse. On one hand, it can drive us to achieve excellence and strive for the best possible outcomes. On the other hand, it can become a source of stress and hinder our progress. In this subchapter, we will explore the concept of perfectionism and discuss strategies to effectively deal with it.

Perfectionism is the belief that everything must be flawless and without any errors. While it may seem like a positive trait, it often leads to a fear of failure and a constant need for validation. This mindset can be paralyzing, preventing us from taking risks and exploring new ideas.

To overcome perfectionism, it is important to adopt a growth mindset, as explained in the book "Mindset: The New Psychology of Success." Embracing a growth mindset means understanding that failure is not an endpoint but an opportunity for learning and growth. By reframing mistakes as stepping stones towards improvement, we can overcome the fear of failure and become more open to taking risks.

Another effective strategy is setting realistic expectations. Perfectionists tend to set impossibly high standards for themselves, leading to a never-ending cycle of dissatisfaction. By setting achievable goals and acknowledging that progress is more important than perfection, we can alleviate the pressure we put on ourselves.

Furthermore, it is crucial to practice self-compassion. Perfectionists often criticize themselves harshly, leading to feelings of self-doubt and low self-esteem. By treating ourselves with kindness and understanding, we can develop a healthier relationship with our own achievements and failures.

Additionally, seeking external feedback and support can be beneficial. Perfectionists often struggle with seeking help, fearing that it may indicate weakness or incompetence. However, by seeking feedback from trusted mentors or peers, we can gain valuable insights and perspectives that can enhance our work.

Lastly, embracing imperfection and being comfortable with uncertainty is key. Innovation and breakthrough ideas often arise from embracing ambiguity and exploring uncharted territories. By letting go of the need for perfection and embracing the messy process of creativity, we open ourselves up to new possibilities and opportunities.

In conclusion, perfectionism can hinder our creativity and progress. However, by adopting a growth mindset, setting realistic expectations, practicing self-compassion, seeking feedback, and embracing imperfection, we can effectively deal with perfectionism. By cultivating a mindset that values progress over perfection, we can unlock our creative potential and generate breakthrough ideas.

Overcoming Resistance to Change

In an ever-evolving world, change is the only constant. Yet, many individuals and organizations struggle to embrace change and adapt to new circumstances. This subchapter aims to provide insights and strategies for overcoming resistance to change, based on the principles discussed in the book "The Innovator's Mind: Cultivating Creativity for Breakthrough Ideas," inspired by the niches of "Mindset: The New Psychology of Success."

Change can be intimidating, as it often disrupts routines and challenges established norms. However, it is crucial to recognize that change is an opportunity for growth and innovation. The first step in overcoming resistance to change is developing a growth mindset. This mindset, as discussed in "Mindset: The New Psychology of Success," believes that abilities and intelligence can be developed through dedication and hard work. Embracing a growth mindset helps individuals and organizations view change as a chance to learn, adapt, and improve.

Understanding the reasons behind resistance to change is essential. Fear of the unknown, loss of control, and a sense of uncertainty are common reasons why individuals resist change. By addressing these concerns, leaders can create an environment that fosters trust and open communication. Engaging stakeholders in the change process, providing clear explanations, and involving them in decision-making can alleviate resistance and build support for the proposed changes.

Another effective strategy for overcoming resistance to change is highlighting the benefits. People are more likely to embrace change if they understand how it will positively impact their lives or the organization. Clearly articulating the reasons and potential advantages of the proposed change can help individuals see the value in embracing it.

Furthermore, providing support and resources during the transition is crucial. Change can be overwhelming, and individuals may require assistance to adapt successfully. Offering training programs, mentorship, and coaching can help individuals develop the necessary skills and confidence to navigate the change effectively.

Lastly, celebrating small wins along the way can motivate individuals and reinforce the benefits of change. Recognizing and acknowledging progress boosts morale and encourages continued efforts towards embracing change.

In conclusion, overcoming resistance to change is vital for personal and organizational growth. By cultivating a growth mindset, understanding the reasons behind resistance, highlighting the benefits, providing support, and celebrating progress, individuals and organizations can successfully navigate the challenges of change. With an open mindset and a willingness to adapt, one can embrace change as an opportunity for innovation and breakthrough ideas, as advocated in "The Innovator's Mind: Cultivating Creativity for Breakthrough Ideas."

Chapter 8: Sustaining Creativity: Building Habits for Long-Term Innovation

Embracing Lifelong Learning

In today's fast-paced and ever-changing world, the concept of lifelong learning has become more important than ever before. The ability to adapt, grow, and acquire new knowledge and skills is no longer a luxury but a necessity for success. In this subchapter, we will explore the significance of embracing lifelong learning and how it can cultivate creativity and foster breakthrough ideas.

The Innovator's Mind: Cultivating Creativity for Breakthrough Ideas acknowledges that the traditional notion of success is no longer solely determined by intelligence or talent. Instead, it emphasizes the importance of having a growth mindset, which is the belief that abilities and intelligence can be developed through dedication and hard work. This mindset is closely tied to the concept of lifelong learning.

Lifelong learning goes beyond the boundaries of formal education. It is a continuous process of acquiring knowledge, skills, and experiences throughout one's life. It involves being open to new ideas, seeking out challenges, and constantly pushing the limits of one's abilities. By embracing lifelong learning, individuals can stay relevant in a rapidly changing world and unlock their creative potential.

One of the key benefits of lifelong learning is that it fosters innovation and creativity. When we expose ourselves to new ideas, perspectives, and experiences, we broaden our horizons and expand our thinking. This allows us to make connections between seemingly unrelated concepts and come up with breakthrough ideas. Lifelong learners are more likely to think outside the box, challenge the status quo, and find unique solutions to problems.

Moreover, embracing lifelong learning leads to personal and professional growth. It enables individuals to adapt to new technologies, industries, and job requirements. Lifelong learners are more versatile, adaptable, and resilient in the face of change. They are not afraid to take risks and step out of their comfort zones, knowing that failure is an opportunity for growth and learning.

In conclusion, embracing lifelong learning is essential for cultivating creativity and achieving breakthrough ideas. It allows individuals to develop a growth mindset, stay relevant in a rapidly changing world, and unlock their creative potential. By embracing lifelong learning, we can adapt to new challenges, grow personally and professionally, and become innovative problem solvers. So, let us embark on a journey of lifelong learning and embrace the opportunities it presents.

Developing a Growth Mindset

In today's rapidly changing world, success is no longer solely dependent on innate talent or intelligence. Instead, it is the mindset we adopt that plays a crucial role in our ability to overcome challenges, adapt to new situations, and ultimately achieve our goals. In this subchapter, we will delve into the concept of developing a growth mindset, as outlined in the book "Mindset: The New Psychology of Success," and explore how it can be applied to foster creativity and innovation.

A growth mindset, as opposed to a fixed mindset, is characterized by the belief that our abilities and intelligence can be developed through dedication, hard work, and a willingness to learn. This mindset embraces challenges, views failures as opportunities for growth, and seeks out feedback as a means of improvement. By understanding the power of a growth mindset, we can unlock our full potential and cultivate creativity for breakthrough ideas.

One of the key aspects of developing a growth mindset is embracing challenges. Rather than shying away from difficult tasks, individuals with a growth mindset see them as opportunities to learn and develop new skills. They understand that by stepping outside of their comfort zones, they can expand their abilities and push the boundaries of what they thought was possible.

Furthermore, a growth mindset views failures as stepping stones to success. Instead of being discouraged by setbacks, individuals with this mindset see them as valuable learning experiences. They analyze their mistakes, identify areas for improvement, and use this feedback to refine their approach. By reframing failure as a natural part of the learning process, they are able to bounce back stronger and more resilient.

Moreover, developing a growth mindset entails seeking out feedback and being open to constructive criticism. Rather than taking feedback personally, individuals with a growth mindset see it as an opportunity to grow and improve. They actively seek input from others, value different perspectives, and use feedback to refine their ideas and strategies.

In conclusion, developing a growth mindset is essential for cultivating creativity and innovation. By embracing challenges, viewing failures as opportunities for growth, and seeking out feedback, we can continuously develop our abilities and achieve breakthrough ideas. Whether you are an aspiring entrepreneur, a student, or a professional in any field, adopting a growth mindset will empower you to navigate the ever-changing landscape and unlock your full potential.

Establishing Creative Rituals and Practices

In the fast-paced world we live in today, cultivating creativity can be a challenge. However, with the right mindset and dedication to establishing creative rituals and practices, anyone can tap into their innate ability to generate breakthrough ideas. In this subchapter, we will explore proven techniques and strategies to help you foster a creative mindset and unlock your full creative potential.

One of the first steps in establishing creative rituals is to create a conducive environment. Surround yourself with inspiration by curating a space that reflects your interests and fuels your creativity. Fill it with books, artwork, and other objects that spark your imagination. This environment will serve as a constant reminder to stay focused on your creative goals.

Another important aspect of establishing creative rituals is setting aside dedicated time for creative activities. Just as athletes have a training schedule, creative individuals need to allocate time for their craft. Whether it's writing, painting, or experimenting with new ideas, make it a habit to engage in creative activities regularly. This consistency will help you develop a creative flow and ensure that you are making progress towards your goals.

Furthermore, incorporating mindfulness practices into your creative rituals can greatly enhance your ability to generate breakthrough ideas. Mindfulness allows you to be fully present and aware of your thoughts and emotions, creating a fertile ground for creativity to flourish. Incorporate techniques such as meditation, deep breathing exercises, or journaling to cultivate a calm and focused state of mind.

Collaboration is also key in establishing creative rituals and practices. Surround yourself with like-minded individuals who share your passion for creativity. Engage in brainstorming sessions, workshops, or join creative communities to share ideas and gain fresh perspectives. Collaborative efforts not only enhance creativity but also foster a supportive network that can help you strive for breakthrough ideas.

Lastly, don't be afraid to embrace failure as part of the creative process. Creativity requires experimentation and taking risks. Learn from your mistakes, iterate, and keep pushing boundaries. By adopting a growth mindset and viewing failures as opportunities for growth, you will be able to overcome obstacles and ultimately achieve your creative goals.

Establishing creative rituals and practices is crucial for cultivating a creative mindset. By creating a conducive environment, dedicating time for creative activities, incorporating mindfulness practices, fostering collaboration, and embracing failure, anyone can tap into their creative potential and generate breakthrough ideas. So, start today and unlock your inner innovator!

Nurturing a Supportive Network

In the journey towards cultivating creativity and generating breakthrough ideas, it is crucial to recognize the significance of nurturing a supportive network. As humans, we are inherently social beings, and our connections with others can greatly influence our mindset and success. In this subchapter, we will explore the power of a supportive network and how it contributes to developing an innovator's mind.

A supportive network consists of individuals who not only believe in your potential but also encourage and inspire you to explore your creative potential. These individuals can be friends, family members, mentors, or even colleagues who share your passion for innovation. They are the ones who provide a safe space for you to take risks, share ideas, and receive constructive feedback.

One of the primary benefits of a supportive network is the opportunity for collaboration. When you surround yourself with like-minded individuals, you create a synergy that fuels your creativity. Through collaboration, you can bounce ideas off each other, challenge assumptions, and gain new perspectives. This collaborative environment fosters an atmosphere of continuous learning and growth, pushing you to think outside the box and explore unconventional approaches.

Moreover, a supportive network serves as a pillar of emotional support. Pursuing breakthrough ideas can be daunting, and setbacks are inevitable. During these challenging times, having a network that believes in your abilities and provides encouragement can make all the difference. They help you navigate through obstacles, provide guidance, and remind you of your strengths when self-doubt creeps in.

In addition to emotional support, a supportive network can also open doors to new opportunities. Your connections may have access to resources, expertise, or networks that can propel your ideas forward. By leveraging these connections, you can expand your reach, gain valuable insights, and increase the likelihood of success.

To nurture a supportive network, it is essential to cultivate strong relationships based on trust, respect, and reciprocity. Actively seek out individuals who share your passion for innovation and invest time and effort in fostering those relationships. Attend networking events, join communities or organizations centered around creativity and innovation, and engage in meaningful conversations with individuals who inspire you.

In conclusion, nurturing a supportive network is a vital aspect of cultivating an innovator's mind. Surrounding yourself with individuals who believe in your potential, encourage collaboration, provide emotional support, and open doors to opportunities can significantly enhance your creative journey. So, take the time to invest in these relationships, for they are the foundation upon which breakthrough ideas are built.

Chapter 9: Applying Creativity and Innovation in Different Fields

Creativity in Business and Entrepreneurship

Creativity is often seen as an elusive quality, reserved for artists, musicians, and writers. However, in today's rapidly changing and competitive business landscape, creativity has become a vital skill that any entrepreneur or business professional must possess. In this subchapter, we will explore the importance of creativity in business and entrepreneurship, and how fostering a creative mindset can lead to breakthrough ideas and success.

In the book "The Innovator's Mind: Cultivating Creativity for Breakthrough Ideas," we delve into the concept of creativity from a business perspective and how it can be harnessed to drive innovation, solve complex problems, and inspire new ways of thinking.

First and foremost, it is important to understand that creativity is not limited to a select few individuals. It is a skill that can be developed and nurtured through deliberate practice and a growth mindset. By adopting a mindset focused on continuous learning and embracing challenges, entrepreneurs can unlock their creative potential and generate innovative solutions to the problems they encounter.

One of the key aspects of fostering creativity in business is creating an environment that encourages and rewards creative thinking. This includes promoting a culture of openness, where ideas are valued regardless of their source, and encouraging collaboration and diverse perspectives. By embracing diversity and incorporating different viewpoints, entrepreneurs can tap into a wealth of ideas and insights that can lead to breakthrough innovations.

Another crucial element in cultivating creativity is the ability to think outside the box. This involves challenging conventional wisdom, questioning assumptions, and exploring new possibilities. By pushing boundaries and taking calculated risks, entrepreneurs can discover new opportunities and disrupt existing industries.

Moreover, creativity in business is not just about generating ideas; it also involves the ability to execute those ideas effectively. Entrepreneurs must have the resilience and determination to push through obstacles and bring their innovative ideas to fruition. This requires them to embrace failure as a learning opportunity and persevere in the face of setbacks.

In conclusion, creativity is a vital skill for success in business and entrepreneurship. By cultivating a creative mindset, entrepreneurs can unlock their true potential and generate breakthrough ideas that can transform industries. Through fostering a culture of openness, embracing diversity, and thinking outside the box, entrepreneurs can harness the power of creativity to drive innovation and achieve their goals. So, whether you are an aspiring entrepreneur or an established business professional, embracing creativity is the key to unlocking your success in the ever-changing world of business.

Creativity in Science and Technology

In the ever-evolving fields of science and technology, creativity plays a vital role in driving breakthrough ideas and innovations. It is no longer sufficient to rely solely on technical expertise and knowledge; a creative mindset is now recognized as a key component for success in these fields. This subchapter explores the importance of creativity in science and technology and provides insights into how to cultivate and harness it effectively.

Creativity is the ability to generate novel and valuable ideas. In the context of science and technology, it involves thinking outside the box, challenging existing paradigms, and finding innovative solutions to complex problems. In a rapidly changing world, where new challenges continuously arise, creative thinking is essential to stay ahead of the curve.

One of the reasons creativity is integral to science and technology is that it enables researchers and engineers to connect seemingly unrelated concepts and ideas, leading to groundbreaking discoveries. By combining different perspectives, disciplines, and approaches, creative thinkers can uncover new insights and pioneer transformative technologies.

Additionally, creativity allows scientists and technologists to embrace failure and learn from it. Experimentation and trial-and-error are essential components of the creative process. Rather than seeing failure as a setback, creative individuals view it as an opportunity to refine their ideas and approaches. This mindset fosters resilience and perseverance, crucial traits for success in the face of challenges and setbacks.

To cultivate creativity in science and technology, individuals must adopt a growth mindset. This mindset, as explored in the book "Mindset: The New Psychology of Success," emphasizes the belief that abilities and intelligence can be developed through dedication and effort. By embracing this mindset, scientists and technologists can overcome self-doubt and fear of failure, enabling them to take risks and explore new possibilities.

Furthermore, creating an environment that fosters creativity is essential. Encouraging collaboration, diversity of thought, and open communication channels can stimulate the exchange of ideas and nurture innovation. Providing resources and support for ongoing learning and professional development is also crucial for cultivating a creative culture in science and technology.

In conclusion, creativity is a driving force in the fields of science and technology. It enables individuals to generate novel ideas, connect seemingly unrelated concepts, and overcome challenges. By embracing a growth mindset and creating an environment that fosters creativity, scientists and technologists can unleash their full potential and contribute to breakthrough discoveries and innovations.

Creativity in Arts and Design

In today's rapidly changing world, creativity has become a crucial skill for success in various fields, particularly in arts and design. The ability to think outside the box and come up with innovative ideas is not only sought after but also necessary for individuals to thrive in the competitive landscape. This subchapter delves into the realm of creativity in arts and design, exploring its significance, methods, and the mindset required to cultivate it.

Art and design are more than just aesthetic expressions; they are powerful means of communication and vehicles for innovation. Creativity plays a pivotal role in these fields, enabling artists and designers to challenge conventions, question norms, and push boundaries. It is through creativity that new artistic movements, groundbreaking designs, and thought-provoking visual narratives are born.

To foster creativity in arts and design, it is essential to embrace a growth mindset – a concept introduced by psychologist Carol Dweck in her book "Mindset: The New Psychology of Success." A growth mindset emphasizes the belief that abilities and talents can be developed through dedication, hard work, and a willingness to learn. By adopting this mindset, individuals open themselves up to endless possibilities, allowing their creativity to flourish.

This subchapter delves into various techniques and strategies that can enhance creativity in arts and design. It explores brainstorming exercises, divergent thinking, and the power of embracing failure as a stepping stone towards progress. Additionally, it highlights the significance of multidisciplinary collaboration and the value of seeking inspiration from diverse sources.

Furthermore, this subchapter emphasizes the importance of cultivating an environment that nurtures creativity. It discusses the role of curiosity, playfulness, and experimentation in sparking innovative ideas. It also explores the relationship between creativity and mindfulness, suggesting that being present in the moment can enhance the creative process.

Ultimately, this subchapter aims to inspire individuals from any background to embrace their creative potential and explore the limitless possibilities within arts and design. By understanding the role of mindset, techniques, and environmental factors in cultivating creativity, readers can unlock their own imaginative powers and contribute to the ever-evolving landscape of artistic expression and design innovation.

Creativity in Education and Learning

Introduction:

In today's rapidly changing world, education and learning play a crucial role in shaping individuals' future success. However, traditional educational systems often focus on rote memorization and standardized testing, leaving little room for creativity. Recognizing the need to cultivate creativity in education, this subchapter delves into the importance of creativity in the learning process and its impact on personal growth and innovation. Drawing inspiration from "The Innovator's Mind: Cultivating Creativity for Breakthrough Ideas" and Carol Dweck's "Mindset: The New Psychology of Success," this chapter explores the power of a creative mindset in education.

The Power of Creativity in Education: Creativity is an essential skill that empowers individuals to think outside the box, solve complex problems, and adapt to new challenges. It encourages students to question, explore, and experiment, fostering a deep understanding of concepts and promoting critical thinking skills. By integrating creativity into the learning process, students can unleash their imaginations, develop innovative ideas, and become more engaged in their education.

Nurturing a Creative Mindset: Carol Dweck's groundbreaking research on mindset highlights the importance of cultivating a growth mindset in education. A growth mindset enables individuals to embrace challenges, persevere through setbacks, and believe in their ability to learn and grow. By encouraging students to adopt a growth mindset, educators can create an environment that encourages risk-taking, curiosity, and creativity.

This mindset not only enhances students' academic achievements but also equips them with the skills necessary for success in the future.

Integrating Creativity Across Disciplines: Creativity should not be limited to artistic or creative subjects. It should be integrated across all disciplines, including math, science, and humanities. By infusing creativity into various subjects, educators can facilitate interdisciplinary thinking and encourage students to approach problems from different angles. This approach fosters innovation, as students learn to connect seemingly unrelated concepts and apply creative problem-solving techniques to real-world scenarios.

Promoting Collaboration and Communication: Creativity is often nurtured through collaboration and effective communication. By incorporating group projects, brainstorming sessions, and open discussions, educators can create an environment that promotes collaboration and allows students to share ideas and perspectives. Through these interactions, students develop empathy, learn to appreciate diverse viewpoints, and enhance their creative thinking abilities.

Conclusion:

Creativity in education and learning is crucial for nurturing individuals' ability to think innovatively, adapt to change, and contribute to society. By embracing creativity, educators can empower students to become lifelong learners, critical thinkers, and problem solvers. Whether in the arts, sciences, or any other discipline, a creative mindset fosters personal growth, enhances academic achievements, and cultivates the next generation of innovators.

Chapter 10: The Future of Creativity and Innovation

Emerging Trends and Technologies

In today's rapidly evolving world, it has become essential to stay updated with the latest emerging trends and technologies. The Innovator's Mind: Cultivating Creativity for Breakthrough Ideas is here to guide you through this dynamic landscape. Whether you are a student, professional, or entrepreneur, understanding the emerging trends and technologies is crucial to achieving success in the modern age.

The subchapter "Emerging Trends and Technologies" delves into the exciting developments that are shaping various industries and transforming the way we live, work, and communicate. This chapter aims to provide you with valuable insights and perspectives to help you navigate these advancements effectively.

One of the most significant trends discussed in this subchapter is the rise of artificial intelligence (AI) and machine learning (ML). These technologies have the potential to revolutionize numerous sectors, from healthcare and finance to transportation and entertainment. By understanding the possibilities and limitations of AI and ML, you can leverage these tools to enhance productivity, improve decision-making, and drive innovation.

Another important trend covered in this subchapter is the Internet of Things (IoT). With the increasing interconnectivity of devices, IoT is opening up new avenues for data collection, analysis, and automation. By harnessing the power of IoT, businesses can optimize their operations, create personalized experiences for customers, and unlock untapped opportunities for growth.

Furthermore, this subchapter explores the impact of blockchain technology. Originally associated with cryptocurrencies, blockchain has now expanded its applications to areas such as supply chain management, digital identity verification, and decentralized finance. By understanding the fundamentals of blockchain, you can develop forward-thinking strategies that leverage its security, transparency, and efficiency.

Additionally, the subchapter touches upon trends like 5G technology, augmented reality (AR), and virtual reality (VR). These technologies are poised to redefine communication, entertainment, and immersive experiences. By staying informed about these emerging trends, you can position yourself as an early adopter and gain a competitive edge in your field.

In conclusion, "Emerging Trends and Technologies" is a subchapter that offers a comprehensive overview of the latest developments shaping our world. By cultivating an understanding of these trends and technologies, you can embrace innovation, adapt to change, and unlock breakthrough ideas. Whether you are a student seeking to shape your career path or a professional aiming to stay ahead of the curve, this subchapter will equip you with the knowledge and mindset necessary to thrive in the ever-evolving landscape of emerging trends and technologies.

The Role of Artificial Intelligence in Creativity

In the modern world, the advent of artificial intelligence (AI) has revolutionized various aspects of our lives, including the creative process. Traditionally, creativity has been seen as a distinctly human attribute, but with the advancements in AI technology, we are witnessing its emergence as an invaluable tool in the creative realm. This subchapter explores the role of AI in creativity and how it is transforming the way we approach innovative thinking.

AI has the capability to analyze vast amounts of data, identify patterns, and generate insights that can fuel the creative process. It can assist creatives by providing them with inspiration, generating ideas, and even creating original content. By harnessing AI's computational power, individuals can overcome creative blocks and tap into a wealth of possibilities that were previously inaccessible.

One area where AI has made significant contributions is in the field of art. AI algorithms can analyze patterns in existing artwork, learn from them, and generate new pieces that mimic the style and techniques of renowned artists. This has not only expanded the boundaries of artistic expression but also challenged our understanding of what it means to create art. AI-powered tools have become indispensable for artists seeking to explore new frontiers and push the boundaries of their creativity.

AI is also transforming the advertising and marketing industry. By analyzing vast amounts of consumer data, AI algorithms can create personalized and targeted campaigns that resonate with specific audiences. This level of personalization not only enhances the effectiveness of marketing efforts but also allows for more creative and engaging content creation.

Moreover, AI-powered tools are aiding in the development of breakthrough ideas in fields such as product design, architecture, and even scientific research. By leveraging AI's ability to process and analyze complex data, researchers and designers can gain new insights and explore innovative solutions. This collaboration between human creativity and AI's computational power is leading to groundbreaking discoveries and advancements in various fields.

However, it is important to note that while AI can enhance the creative process, it cannot replace human creativity. AI is a tool that complements and augments human ingenuity, but it is the human mind that ultimately drives the creative process. The interaction between AI and human creativity opens up new possibilities, challenges traditional notions, and fosters a mindset of continuous innovation.

In conclusion, the role of artificial intelligence in creativity is transformative. AI's ability to analyze data, generate insights, and mimic creative processes has revolutionized various industries. It has expanded the boundaries of artistic expression, fueled breakthrough ideas in research and design, and enhanced marketing and advertising efforts. However, it is crucial to remember that AI is a tool that supports human creativity rather than replacing it. By embracing AI and cultivating a mindset of continuous innovation, we can harness the power of technology to unlock our creative potential and achieve breakthrough ideas.

Ethical Considerations in Innovation

Innovation has become a driving force in our rapidly evolving world. It fuels progress, fosters growth, and propels societies forward. However, in the pursuit of groundbreaking ideas and breakthroughs, it is essential to recognize and address the ethical considerations that emerge along the way. This subchapter titled "Ethical Considerations in Innovation" from the book "The Innovator's Mind: Cultivating Creativity for Breakthrough Ideas" delves into the importance of integrating ethical perspectives into the innovation process.

The chapter begins by emphasizing the significance of ethics in innovation. It explores how the mindset of innovators plays a crucial role in determining the ethical implications of their creations. By cultivating a mindset that prioritizes ethical considerations, innovators can ensure that their innovations align with principles of integrity, responsibility, and social good.

The subchapter goes on to explore various ethical dilemmas that innovators may face. It addresses issues such as privacy, data security, and the potential societal impacts of emerging technologies. With real-life examples, it highlights the need for innovators to navigate these challenges while upholding ethical standards and avoiding harm to individuals and communities.

Furthermore, the chapter offers practical guidance on how innovators can integrate ethical considerations into their creative process. It emphasizes the importance of conducting thorough research, engaging in cross-disciplinary collaboration, and seeking diverse perspectives. By involving stakeholders and considering the potential consequences of their innovations, innovators can proactively address ethical concerns and mitigate risks.

The subchapter also emphasizes the role of regulation and public policy in promoting ethical innovation. It explores the need for transparent and accountable governance frameworks that guide innovation practices. By adhering to regulatory guidelines and embracing ethical principles, innovators can build trust with their users, consumers, and wider society.

Finally, the subchapter concludes by highlighting the benefits of ethical innovation. It showcases how ethical considerations can enhance the reputation and sustainability of innovative ventures. By prioritizing social impact, environmental responsibility, and fairness, innovators can create a positive legacy and contribute to a more inclusive and equitable future.

This subchapter "Ethical Considerations in Innovation" from "The Innovator's Mind: Cultivating Creativity for Breakthrough Ideas" serves as a thought-provoking guide for anyone interested in the intersection of innovation and ethics. It provides valuable insights and practical strategies to ensure that innovation serves the greater good while upholding ethical standards.

Cultivating Creativity for a Sustainable Future

In today's rapidly changing world, creativity has become a crucial skill for individuals and organizations alike. The ability to think outside the box and generate innovative solutions has never been more important. In this subchapter, we will explore how cultivating creativity can lead us towards a sustainable future.

Creativity is not limited to artists or musicians; it is a mindset that anyone can develop. In "The Innovator's Mind: Cultivating Creativity for Breakthrough Ideas," we delve into the psychology of success and how a growth mindset can foster creativity. By understanding the power of our mindset, we can unlock our creative potential and make a positive impact on the world.

Creativity is essential for addressing the complex challenges we face today, such as climate change, poverty, and social inequality. We need fresh perspectives and unconventional approaches to find sustainable solutions. By cultivating our creativity, we can think beyond existing paradigms and explore new possibilities.

One key aspect of cultivating creativity is embracing failure and learning from it. Often, fear of failure holds us back from taking risks and venturing into uncharted territory. However, failure is an integral part of the creative process. By reframing failure as an opportunity for growth and learning, we can overcome obstacles and foster innovation.

Another important aspect is nurturing curiosity and a sense of wonder. Children are naturally curious, but as we grow older, we often lose that sense of awe and exploration. By rekindling our curiosity, we can open ourselves up to new experiences and ideas. Engaging in activities that spark our curiosity, such as traveling, reading, or attending workshops, can enhance our creative thinking.

Furthermore, collaboration is vital for cultivating creativity. By connecting with others and embracing diverse perspectives, we can expand our thinking and generate breakthrough ideas. Building a creative community where ideas can be shared and refined fosters an environment conducive to innovation.

Finally, creativity requires time and space for reflection. In our fast-paced world, it is easy to get caught up in the busyness of daily life. Taking the time to pause, reflect, and recharge is essential for nurturing our creative minds. Whether through meditation, journaling, or simply spending time in nature, creating space for introspection allows us to tap into our creative potential.

In conclusion, cultivating creativity is not just a personal endeavor but a collective responsibility for shaping a sustainable future. By adopting a growth mindset, embracing failure, nurturing curiosity, fostering collaboration, and creating space for reflection, we can unlock our creative potential and generate breakthrough ideas. Let us embark on this journey together, cultivating creativity for a brighter and more sustainable future.

Conclusion: Cultivating Your Innovator's Mind

In this journey towards cultivating your innovator's mind, we have explored the depths of creativity and its power to generate breakthrough ideas. Throughout this book, "The Innovator's Mind: Cultivating Creativity for Breakthrough Ideas," we have delved into the realm of mindset and how it plays a crucial role in achieving success.

Mindset: The New Psychology of Success has become a fundamental concept that has revolutionized the way we approach challenges and embrace opportunities. It is the driving force behind our ability to think outside the box, discover new possibilities, and make a lasting impact in our personal and professional lives.

Throughout these pages, we have witnessed the transformative power of adopting a growth mindset. We have learned that intelligence and talent are not fixed traits, but rather qualities that can be developed through dedication, perseverance, and a passion for learning. By cultivating a growth mindset, we open ourselves up to endless possibilities and become more resilient in the face of obstacles.

One of the key takeaways from this book is the understanding that failure is not the end, but an opportunity for growth and learning. By embracing failure as a stepping stone towards success, we can unlock our full potential and unleash our inner innovators. It is through the process of trial and error that we refine our ideas, challenge the status quo, and ultimately create breakthrough innovations.

To cultivate an innovator's mind, we must also embrace curiosity and embrace the unknown. By constantly asking questions, seeking new knowledge, and exploring diverse perspectives, we expand our creative horizons and ignite the spark of innovation. We must be open to change, adaptable to new circumstances, and willing to take risks.

In conclusion, cultivating your innovator's mind is a lifelong journey. It requires dedication, resilience, and a commitment to continuous learning. By adopting a growth mindset, embracing failure, and nurturing curiosity, you can unleash your creative potential and bring forth groundbreaking ideas that shape the world around you.

Remember, the power to innovate lies within each and every one of us. Embrace the challenges, overcome the obstacles, and dare to dream big. Cultivate your innovator's mind and pave the way for a future filled with breakthrough ideas and endless possibilities.

Are you ready to embark on this transformative journey towards cultivating your innovator's mind? The choice is yours.